DOWN BY THE RIVERSIDE

DOWN BY THE RIVERSIDE

December Scorpio Moon Publishing

Down By The Riverside

By Tamara Angela

Copyright 2023 December Scorpio Moon Publishing

ISBN Paperback: 979-8-9860980-0-5

ISBN Digital: 979-8-9860980-1-2

This novel is entirely a work of fiction. The names, characters and incidents portrayed in it are the work of the author's imagination. Any resemblance to actual persons, living or dead, events or localities is entirely coincidental.

1

Down By The Riverside

Does God ever come to Cottonbound, Mississippi?

There was a time that the people there called for Her endlessly.

She came that one day. On the banks of the river, where one of her sons swam across the veil.

The water was so glorious, so warm, so beautifully clear that day, that Jordan didn't even know when he'd left the banks of the riverside near his grandmother's house and swam ashore to The Other Side.

"Jordan. Come on out of the water now, Jordan."

She stood there in all of her power, golden slippers and a starry crown in her hands as she beckoned him from the waters. He wasn't listening but She knew that he heard Her as he floated effortlessly on his back, face up to the rising sun.

"It feels good in here. A few more minutes please," he asked.

She sighed.

"Time isn't a thing here. You will soon get used to that. Go ahead."

Jordan watched as God stood vigilant at the shore as he dove deeper into the waters. His grandmother had always told him that God was patient and kind. So surely God would let him take one more lap in the waters of the river, right?

Diving deeper, there was a silence. A vacuum. No splash.

A weightlessness took over. Enveloped Jordan. Made him feel comfortable as he floated back toward the surface, following the light.

"Okay, I'm ready," he said as he came ashore. He'd swam in this river his entire life. But today, the trees swayed differently. The sun was a bit brighter. He couldn't help but to notice a branch from the old poplar tree that had been there for generations, laying broken on the ground. The sight of that branch sent a pang through his body.

"Come my child. Let's take a walk." God gave him a robe, the slippers, and the crown.

Jordan couldn't keep his eyes off of the branch. His body wanted to buckle under the weight of something unknown.

God would have the answers for certain.

"My grandmother is going to come looking for me. I should let her know where I am. I don't need any smoke from her." Wrapping the robe around his shoulders, Jordan felt a jolt to his system.

"Willa knows where you are, Jordan. Come walk with me."

Everything was familiar, but then it wasn't. Peaceful with an undercurrent of war.

You couldn't *not* go where God was leading you, so Jordan put the slippers on his feet and walked at God's side.

Her words were calming. Her presence reinforcing as Jordan soon came to see that it was only him and God there in that peaceful place.

Music played from the church where Jordan had gone to service his entire life. He hummed along. "My grandmother played this song every Sunday before service. I always wanted to know what a life was like where you didn't have to study war no more. Seems like we have to study war to fight with Love. At least that's what I told my grandmother. She says that ain't the way it's 'sposed to be. We gotta lay down our weapons to get to a place of Love. I told her that we gotta use those weapons 'til Love is staring us in the face, with no outside threats. And so far, I ain't seen a life like that."

"You're both right in a way. I meant for life to be filled with Love. Peace. Joy. There were some that took it upon themselves to change that all on their own. Go against the design. I trust that my children will get back to the design. I never changed the blueprint. It still exists. But I can't force it on y'all. Well, sometimes I exert myself, but in order for it to stick, y'all have to choose it. I want y'all to choose Love, and then only war when necessary."

Jordan paused for a moment as the melodies rained down, floating on the wind.

"No one chose Love when they hanged my daddy from that there poplar tree. Strung him up like a stuck pig and let his body twirl 'round til that branch broke and the maggots came for him. They chose war that day. Dared us to come collect him. He stunk to high heaven when we could finally get his body. A piece of my grandmother died along with him that day. Buried right there in the ground. Three pieces of me left with him."

"Three?" God asked.

"Yes, Ma'am. Three. My heart, my mind, and the ability to think peacefully first."

"Ah, well now. I can understand that, my Son."

"Do you really? Because I heard my grandmother call for you so many times in the middle of the night, on her knees, calling out. 'Til I had to tell her that God don't come down to Cottonbound. God ain't coming down here. Not for us. God ain't showed up not-a once when all those Black bodies hung from the trees over the years. Not when them white folks shot Pearl Ray's husband Luther dead in the street. Said he stole an apple from the grocer. Good man dying over a piece of fruit and a lie. Where was God when they raped Annie Lee and left her for dead? She was going to go away to Atlanta to college, make something of herself. 'Stead, she sit in the back of her mama's house, clambering away, mumbling all the time about nonsense. Rocking back and forth. Ain't been right since! Do you go at night and whisper in Annie Lee's ear? Do her mama's prayers ever reach you, God? I ain't never seent you here in Cottonbound. Not-a once."

"Are you done, Son?"

"No. I'm not. Now that I've got your attention, I got things to say. You said we gone walk and talk, so let's gone and talk. Talk about this life of ours, this life of mine. Since you seem to got time." Jordan's chest heaved with frustration, and for a moment, he paused briefly because he knew that if his grandmother ever heard him talking to God like that, she would grab him by the arm and pinch him silently real good.

God nodded calmly. "We have nothing but time, Jordan. And just to let you know, I was there through all of the things you mentioned."

"Tuh. If you say so. I just can't make any of it make any sense. It's supposed to make sense."

"Who says that it should? The way humans are made, they have choices. Some make good ones. Some don't." God stopped, seeming to marvel at a bird that flew past the two of them. Jordan wondered how there could be such a moment of content in the midst of a conversation that was so full of strife.

He thought of all of the Bible study he'd done with his grandmother. How much he'd sat in that small church and listened to the pastor give a word on what life was supposed to be like. Grandmother even had Pastor over for dinner many times. Countless prayers. Time spent alone on her knees in the prayer closet. Calling for Jesus. Begging God to change things. Sometimes there was change. Sometimes there wasn't.

What was the point of it all?

As they neared the church, things got a bit blurry. Ripples filtered through Jordan's body.

"We have to stop right here, Jordan. Can't really go any further. Too much sorrow over that-a-way. We can't let it suck you in. Could be harmful to you and others."

They stopped walking. A wave of emotion crashed over Jordan, only to stop as quickly as it started. He could hear everything all at once. It was crystal clear. Magnified. Everything was magnified. The scent of the magnolia from the trees across the river. The powdery scent of his grandmother's perfume. The sandpaper-like sound of her voice. The warmth of the sun. The taste of fresh fried catfish and a side of coleslaw. The sight of the sun setting over the river. There was a time when he thought God had known about them in Cottonbound, because all of these things existed.

"Is this where it all stops?" There was a sudden knowing that came over him.

"What do you mean, Son?"

"This?" Jordan threw his hands up, looking around. "Is this the last stop? After-," His pause was filled with a knowing.

"Well. Yes, and no. This is the end, but it's also the beginning."

"Both? Now how is that?"

"Yes, Jordan. Both."

"That just don't seem right. Seems like when I went through what I went through, there would be more of a celebration. Matter of fact, ain't someone 'sposed to be here blowing a horn? Some pearly gates or something? My grandmother always said something about the gates, horns, and music and angels or something. Those that passed on meeting you there with open arms. Where is everyone?"

God waited for Jordan to get it all out.

"That's not the way it really works, but if that's what the living want to think and believe, it's fine."

"So is this how it is? You just let things be. Just let them happen? Just stand by as life happens to us humans and let us think all the wrong stuff? I tell you, God. You are something else. And I always wanted to tell you that."

A grin came across God's lips. "I never see it like that, Jordan. I created man in my image. Greatness. Infinite wisdom. Power. Not everyone chooses to see that part. I can't control all of your choices. All of your circumstances. I can't beg you all to notice your purpose and your greatness. Not my job to pull strings on that accord. Man has to deal with all of their choices and it troubles me that the living blame me for all of those choices."

Jordan knelt down, gently running his fingers in the waters of the river as the melodies continued to float on the wind from the church.

"Take for instance, your mother," God continued.

Wincing at the sound of those words, Jordan wanted to stand up and protest loudly. But he sat back down, wanting to hear what God would propose here in reference to his mother.

"Jackie was born a beautiful soul. Beautiful. She grew. She made choices. And I heard your prayers, Jordan. I heard your prayers when she left. I heard your grandmother's prayers when your mother left. Circumstances? Your grandmother was left caring for her grandson. And let me tell you, she never regretted a day of it. She did worry a lot. Her son died tragically, and your mother just up and left. I heard your grandmother's prayers that Jackie would return. I heard *your* prayers that she would return. I heard you both. But did you ever wonder if her not returning *was* the answer to your prayers?"

"How on this earth would keeping a child from his mother ever be the answer to my prayers? That makes no sense."

"It makes perfect sense. You just didn't want to extend into your wisdom to see. I didn't keep you from her. I kept her from you. And you had a mother. You had Willa as a perfect example of what a woman is and how you should be loved. You chose to see what you lost instead of what you gained. Based out of what you thought you would have had. Or should have had. Do you want to know what your mother was doing with her life? Why she wasn't there? Your choice, Jordan."

God presented it all as if the answer was simple.

When was it ever simple?

"Do you want to know? Make a choice."

"Why are you rushing me? You said I had all the time in the world."

"I'm not rushing you. You do have time, but worrying or either tolling too hard isn't what is needed here. You need to choose."

"I want to know."

"Well then, let's go."

God beckoned to Jordan, who held out his hand; half in agreement, half in defiance. They were suddenly floating, untethered. Both somewhere and nowhere all at once. Visions flashed before Jordan. It was almost like going to the picture show. The sight of his parents first meeting took him aback. He'd never known much more than his father had once uttered, "That woman once gave me life with her love before she was the death of me." That was all he'd said. Never offered more. No one mentioned Jackie's name unless Jordan happened to go to the general store and a random person would remark, "Oh now, there is Jackie's child. Growing so nicely!" They would remark as if they planned on themselves giving her the compliment some time soon.

No one ever discussed how she just up and left. How Jordan heard her crying the night before she disappeared. Sobbing on his father's shoulders. Saying something about how she had to pursue her dreams. How she couldn't stay in a place like Cottonbound forever. How her voice was meant to bless people. His father then asked her how she planned on maintaining that blessing when she couldn't stop with snorting the powder.

At the time, Jordan was so young, he didn't know what any of it meant. He hadn't thought about that day since.

The next morning, there was a silent void. Seemed like nothing was moving and no one was breathing. Didn't even hear the rooster crow like usual that morning. His father sat out on the porch, watching the sun come up.

"Son, I don't claim to understand women. Never. I prayed this morning though. Prayed your mama find what she searching for. Pray your Grandmother Willa have strength. Praying for you, my child."

Jordan remembered that moment. His father had prayed for everyone else but himself. What would have happened if he prayed for himself that day? Would God have covered him so he could still be among the living?

The memories flooded back, crisp. A bold sting that hurt in a place deep down that Jordan hadn't known existed. His soul cried out in the vacuum. A visceral moan full of release as more visions became clearer.

Big city. Fast living. Money come. Money go. Loss. Pain. Longing. Having it all and then having nothing at all. Never really finding what she needed at the bottom of the bottle or the tray of blow, but continuing to search anyway. The emptiness was suffocating.

"Enough. I've seen enough." It was time to stop all of it before he saw way too much.

"Knowledge, my Son. Such a privilege and a curse all at once."

Grasping for breath, Jordan closed his eyes and tried to focus on the warmth of the sun.

"We are almost done here. Just a little more."

There was no need to learn more, in Jordan's opinion. He just wanted to move on to his next steps.

"Final stop on this leg of the journey, coming up."

It was worth just leaning all the way in, because Jordan knew that he wouldn't be able to move forward if he didn't.

The immediate silence was beautiful. It was calming as it washed over him. They were standing at the tree.

The tree.

"I'm not ready to talk about this."

"That's fine, Jordan. The longer you take to accept it, the longer it takes to move forward. And forward is the only other option besides staying here in the in between. Way too many souls tarry there."

Sorrow. Anger. Embarrassment. The urge to fight. All washed over him at once.

"How did you let them do that to me?" At first when Jordan asked, the words were spoken almost in a whisper. The rage boiling amplified the question to an earth shattering decibel as he repeated the question over and over.

The only thing that brought a bit of peace was the angels who now stood nearby. White robes, melodies and harmonies, songs balancing on the wind. Their energy enveloping Jordan in a soft, pulsating light. He was there, suspended in air, bathed in the light.

God ascended to where Jordan was, both of them peering down at the tree, the broken branches in disarray on the ground.

God stood by with continued patience.

"Just like how they did my daddy. They did me the same."

For a moment, the skin on Jordan's neck burned. His body shook, his mind raced. A suffocating. A knowing.

A feeling of freedom. Release.

The melodies from the angels did nothing to calm him. Something boiled up from a place deep down inside. He knew that feeling. Anger was a longtime resident in Cottonbound. Jordan and Anger had been well acquainted.

He never knew what to do productively with that acquaintance, so they often walked around tethered, hand in hand.

Screaming never helped. Destroying things never helped. He was too young to drink, but the sips he took of spirits that his father had kept hidden didn't dissolve any of the anger either. Nothing stopped it. Nothing made it subside.

Willa's prayers hadn't covered him, and Jordan knew she'd tried and did the best that she could with all that she had.

That day.

There was an unsettling feeling in the air. But that wasn't unlike most days. There was always something unsettling about being so close to white folks that hated you.

He'd gone to the general store. Something he'd done regularly for his grandmother. She wanted molasses and flour for a cake she was baking that night, and some buttermilk for breakfast in the morning. Walking along the dirt road toward town was uneventful until a raggedy pickup rode by. Kicked up so much dust, he couldn't see directly ahead of him. Trying to dust off his dungarees, he thought about how his grandmother would get after him for wearing his good clothes just to walk to the store. She would have to add these to her wash load and she was sure to fuss about it. Jordan pulled the handkerchief from his back pocket and tried to clear as much of the dust from his clothing as possible. The truck stopped a ways in front of him, then reversed. The dust still flying recklessly.

When the truck stopped in front of him, Jordan peered inside. Three scraggly white men, one with fiery red hair.

"You one of them uppity knee-gras ain't ya? Wiping your clothes down. Like you better'n everyone else. Y'all see this?" The fiery red head seemed to be the ringleader, practically leaning out of the passenger side window.

The driver mashed his foot on the gas while they sat in park, wheels spinning, dirt flying. Jordan held his eyes and mouth closed. Covered his face with the handkerchief so as not to breathe in the dirt and dust. When he heard the driver take his foot off the gas, Jordan said a silent prayer. He'd always been told to call on God. He needed a path out of there. Quickly.

"Way too uppity. Had to take his daddy down a few notches too. Wondering how that Willa raised such high post knee-gras. Would think he would have learned a good lesson with the way they strung his daddy up in that poplar. 'Parently, this one needs a lesson of his own."

By now, the dust was settling and the three men had exited the truck. Jordan tucked his handkerchief back in his pocket and stood his ground without saying a word.

Fear had no place here. Fear would only choke his ability to get out of the impending situation.

"This one mute or somethin'? Make it talk, Harlow. I hear them knee-gras squeal like stuck pigs when you poke 'em," the driver said.

Jordan couldn't decide whether running would change the outcome. Something made him want to stand there. Face it all. Let those white men know that he wasn't a coward. That he saw them. He'd read somewhere that warriors looked their opponents in the eye. Straightaway.

Jordan decided right then that if he moved, it would have to be because they drove off and left him alone, he won the fight, or that they moved his lifeless body from that very spot. They seemed determined to do the latter. He remembered he had his pocket knife.

He'd put that pocket knife to use. Spilled their blood. Made it a point to etch something in each one of them. And they had carried him out of that spot. Moved him all the way to that poplar tree. Suspended him in air on those branches. And as the light faded, Jordan only could recall the feel of the warm water as his body made a splash in the river. He didn't recall anything vividly until he'd woken up on the other side.

The memory fading, Jordan began to focus on the angels who were still serenading. For the first time, things felt calm.

Serene.

"The spirit of a warrior never dies, Jordan. He simply fights his fight, and when that is done, he gets a new assignment."

"I had my whole life ahead of me."

"Remember what I said about time. There is no real measure. You could live until you are 105 and make no impact. Time is all relative. Your work was done."

"I left my grandmother."

"Willa will be fine. Trust me on this."

The melodies increased in volume as a light shone brightly.

"Choices, Jordan. Choices. You made one, based on who you are. A warrior. You've been one in every lifetime. You will get to see that shortly before you choose again how you want your soul to return. I designed you all so that you have choices."

"That light feels warm. Inviting. Those angels still gone be singing where I'm going?"

"Sure are. They are your guides. I suggest you get to know each other well. They've been with you for several lifetimes."

God placed a gentle hand on Jordan's shoulder. "I hope you found your answers, Jordan."

Jordan looked up as God ascended. "Not all the way, but well enough. I do ask you for one thing."

God waited for Jordan's request.

"Please stop by Cottonbound and make sure my grandmother knows that you are there. I feel like she's gonna be lonely for a bit. And since she thinks you two are confidants, it would soothe my mind if you pay her a visit when she says her prayers tonight."

The light was blinding and Jordan knew that it was time to move forward. He said a quick prayer for Cottonbound, Mississippi.

He knew for sure now that God knew where it was on the map.

Hopefully, She would find it in Her heart to stop by.

There were people that needed Her.

A Word On Going Home

~ A word on going home

I've thought for so long on the concept of 'Home'. How some people are so deeply rooted in a place and how some people are completely nomadic. And how all of the above is a strong existence.

When I was about five, my parents moved to Baltimore, MD from Buffalo, NY. I remember they left me in NY with my grandparents to finish Kindergarten while they moved to a new state, new city, and prepared to possibly make a new life. I remember my mother saying that she didn't want to interrupt my schooling or my life if this new city wasn't going to work out. It was my first time understanding that there was a vastness out there outside of what I saw daily. My grandfather took a globe and spun it for me. Showed me that there were all of these different places that existed. People lived in these places and called those places home. He took a map, spread it out on the kitchen table and showed me how to get from Buffalo to Baltimore. When I understood that my grandparents weren't going with me, there was a deep sadness that I had to make sense of because I was excited about the fact that there was a new place to see.

Baltimore is the city that raised me. I spent my formative years there in grade school. The culture is what I carry with me today. When my parents split up, my mother sat me and my sister down and told us that we would not be moving. That she had decided that Baltimore was our home base. It would be the place that we could always return to. For my sister, it was all she knew, being born there. For me, it was all that I knew because I was raised there. All of my associations of what life was like existed in Baltimore. There was such a settling feeling about what my mother was offering us. A root had grown there for us. We didn't have blood ties there as in family, but the friends who we knew, they were our family. We knew those streets. We knew the blocks and everything about how life worked there. She told me that she had thought about going back to Buffalo, but we had been gone for so long, it was no longer home. Although she had pretty much lived there her entire life.

When I prepared to leave and go to Atlanta for college, my mother hugged me and told me that no matter what happened, I could always come home. No matter how life turned out, I should know that I could return here to my roots, that she was happy that I was going to create my own sense of home and that home would be wherever I chose it to be.

I did just that. Came to Atlanta at 17 years old. Ready to see something new. Knowing that people lived a life that I had no clue about. I had gotten to know all about Baltimore and was excited to learn something new. And as life goes, I made a home for myself here in Atlanta. At this point, I have lived in Atlanta longer than I have lived anywhere in my life.

After 27 years, it's home.

But then it's not. Despite birthing my children here, being married then divorced here. Despite knowing these streets like that back of my hand and being deeply immersed in the culture, Baltimore is still my home.

Baltimore is my anchor, my roots still exist there. It's the place that really initiated my soul.

In recent conversation with friends, since so many of us Atlanta residents are technically transplants (at some point in our lives), the question came up about where you call home. The place you are raised, the place you were born, or the place you live? How would one that has moved around in life identify home?

For me the answer is, it's where my roots were planted. Baltimore will always be home. No matter where I travel, visit, or live or how long I haven't lived there. It's funny because my family in Buffalo tell me that Buffalo is home for me. I dispute them because it's not for so many reasons.

Although I was born there, I left when I was about 5 years old. We spent the summers there with my paternal grandparents until I was about 14 or 15 years old. By that time, I didn't want to spend my summer there because I was involved in sports and extracurriculars at home as well as making good money babysitting. I didn't have any friends in Buffalo, never kept in touch with anyone because I hadn't attended grade school or made lasting friendships by the time we moved when I was five. I had cousins and all of my family was there (living and buried), but for me, there were no active roots. Ancestral, but not active, if that makes sense.

Even with Atlanta, I have lived here since 1996. Went to college, had jobs, created a village. I had some family here already and a few friends that I knew from grade school in Baltimore whose families had migrated here in the 90s.

And yet still, when people ask me where I'm from, I say Baltimore, but I live in Atlanta. I can't tell you why there is a need for me to distinguish that. Part of me feels that saying Atlanta is home wipes out the huge part of me that was developed in my rearing in Baltimore. I could also probably say that not calling Atlanta home could make the same argument. I just feel like a Baltimore girl who chose to live in Atlanta.

At any rate, we do choose our home. Whether it's choosing to stay in the place of your birth and build a life into adulthood. Or you make a choice to pack and move and start a new life across the country.

When I had my last suitcase packed, ready for Atlanta, my mother hugged me and said that no matter what, I could always come home. Then right before she passed, she told me that when she leaves this Earth, not to feel especially rooted to one place to the point where I stall myself and don't experience anything else. That wherever I settle and place my heart, and decide to place my head, that would be home. She simply decided to place her heart in Baltimore. A place that she ultimately felt that she belonged. She wanted us to understand that sense of belonging.

Roots. But to know that the tree could grow and expand as far as we saw fit. This may be part of why I don't feel especially tethered, but I do feel rooted. This concept of home comes to me as I do my family tree research for both my maternal and paternal grandfathers.

Home. How one moves from one space to the next and creates roots. How one can be in a place, not of their choosing, and still create a sense of home. And how we have to have this concept that after being in one place for a length of time, a homecoming is necessary.

I haven't really gone home to Baltimore since my mother died in 2006. And yet the roots from my tree still call me there. The calling gets stronger day by day. Soon, I will answer.

Homecoming

Homecoming

Hunted
The scent of blood
lingering in a trail of tears
Memories fade
Washed away by an ocean deep
The grand design
Established so you never tap in again
Silencing all that your molecules know
To be true
Suffocating
The walking dead
Because one day if you remember
Who you are
You might rise up
You might recall how the Universe loved you
How the two of you walked hand in hand
Aura and Starlight
Magic in pure form
Raw
Rare
You might remember that you were strong
Self-sufficient
You might remember
What life was life before you were prey

Before your reflection betrayed you
What life was like before your blood was spilled
When it pumped through your veins on Divine soil
They need you to forget
They need you to walk blindly
Their very existence depends on your believing everything they say
Their existence requires that you forget
They only exist when your blood runs cold
They saw your power all while you forgot it
While your very life force drained from your body,
Left your soul
While the lights went out behind your eyes
They thrived
And they desire immortality
So you must dwell in dark places
Shadows
Cold Blood
Lights out
Soul disconnected
It's been way too long
See, the thing is Mother will always breathe life into those she birthed
Oceans are her lifeline, her source, her power
There are no boundaries between you and Her
She has remained connected
Prana pumping through your veins
Infused in your meridians
Your soul knows
Your soul hears her
Distant echoes tap your heart
Will you listen?
Can you hear her over the volume of the ocean waves?

Can you hear her over the centuries that buried you alive several times over?
She cries for you
Yearns for you
She carried you
Nurtured you
Loved you when you were but a constellation
Mother said you can return to her
Lie in her bosom
Because God knows your soul hasn't had rest
What if you changed the frequency?
Tuned in to the soothing lullabies from beyond
Ear to the ground so you can smell the scent of the earth
Feel Her vibrations lift you
If you are quiet, really still
You can hear the choir singing
Ancestral melodies have always guided us
They set the table
Prepared the feast
You can come home
You aren't lost
Your soul knows the way
Your feet know the direction instinctively through the lands that their blood fertilized
Their tears irrigated that space
Machetes cleared the path
They walked first
Follow where they guide
All you have to do is breathe
Take a step
Feel their blood pulsing through your veins
Be reminded that they never really died

Those whispers you hear?
Let them speak
Let them envelope you and take you higher
Omnipotent guides
They know best
The route to come home

2

Devil's Playground

*Nobody knows for sure what or who you will meet at the crossroads.
'Cept the folks who done been there.*

*And you don't go visit the Devil's Playground for nothing. You go
because your soul is seeking, desperate. Needing change.*

Some call it magic.

Conjure and legend.

*Only even exchanges happen at the crossroads. Decisions have to
be made.*

Bones buried with those dead men who tell no tales.

*Once you go, ain't no turning back. Can't renege and say you don't
want to be there. Too late. You gotta jump, leap.*

Move with the spirit.

Devil don't make backdoor deals. Everything done out in the open.

That's how free will works.

You gotta give something up.

What you got that's worth something to the Devil?

I'm gonna whisper this 'cause it's between me and you.

*Devil will take anything you got. 'Cause to him, if your soul isn't
worth a thing to you, ain't worth a heap of nothing to him either.*

Gone down to the crossroads and give your offering.

That's how it all starts.

They say you can never get something for nothing.

~

God was said to mainly take care of babies and fools.

Memphis didn't believe himself to be either immature or naive. But his mama told him that was who God took care of. So that meant that Memphis had to take care of himself because God may be too busy to pay attention to him. There were ways of care that would be acceptable and ways that were considered not.

He had always leaned towards the latter. Because the former hadn't been working.

Praying wasn't enough to keep food on the table for his mama and sisters and younger brother. They went without way too often. Much too often for Memphis' taste. Couldn't understand how his mama stayed on her knees begging God so much on those nights that their heads hit the pillow and their stomachs would be flat against their backs.

Not enough.

A man had choices.

Memphis had options and he was going to take them, whether his mama and her God liked it or not.

She wasn't too keen on him singing and playing that haint music that he liked so much, so he took another opportunity up his sleeve. Something he was way better at anyway, because really, he loved his mama too much to make her feel disrespected. Disappointment was fine by him though. He had already disappointed her so they were both familiar with that feeling, but he knew that if that disappointment came with money, she would take the money and not worry about the disappointment too much.

The money was going to be huge. He could feel it in his soul. Plus Marie told him what she saw for him. Tons of cash made from those tiny bottles. All he had to do was mix it like she say and boom, he would get paid. Simple. People were buying for sure.

There was magic in the cure.

Marie made sure that Memphis had the cure.

It was what he prayed for at the crossroads and Memphis would be damned if he didn't hop on the chance when it came.

Opportunity staring him in the face as it did that one day he got off the bus in a dusty little town only a few hundred miles from his own. It was as far as the money he had in his pockets at the time would take him. He showed up there with his guitar ready to stand on any corner and play. Change of scenery suited him well anyway

That's when he met Marie.

She stood outside a small storefront with a purple door, staring at him while he sang. He couldn't help but see her. Petite woman, hair in a severe bun piled at the top of her head, purple dress that matched that door. Memphis couldn't remember ever seeing a door to anywhere painted purple.

He made some money that day from the passersby and when he packed up his guitar, he couldn't help but feel the pull to that purple door and the woman in he purple dress. Who was that woman?

He didn't remember walking across the dusty road or entering the small store. He just remembered how the petite woman seemed to appear out of nowhere.

And that she smelled of gardenias.

"Can I help you?" she asked, voice light and sweet.

"Maybe. I don't even know really what brought me in here." Memphis took a moment to look around.

"Usually people breeze through here for a little of this and a little of that. You look like you could use some refreshment though. Been out there performing and such. You sound pretty good, Mister-,"

"Memphis. Name's Memphis. No formalities needed."

"Well you sound pretty good, Memphis. And my name is Marie. It's a pleasure to meet you."

"Pleasure is all mine, Marie. I think I will take you up on that refreshment you offered."

She smiled and told him to be patient while she went to the back. He set his guitar down and browsed. Teas neatly lined the shelves in glass canisters. There were some other things he did not recognize. Bowls with colorful, smooth rocks and vials with liquids.

Marie returned with a tray, two glasses, and a pitcher with chilled refreshment.

"I made a fresh pitcher of passion flower lemonade right before you came. Hope you like it."

"Can't say I have ever had that flavor but it's worth a try with the present company."

"Why don't we go on out on the back porch for a spell? That is, if you aren't busy otherwise."

"As a matter of fact I am not at the present moment. I was planning to stay in town overnight and make it on home with the first train at sunrise."

Memphis followed Marie to the back porch. She took a seat and poured them both a glass of the lemonade. Memphis had never tasted anything like it and before he knew it, they had both finished the pitcher over easy flowing conversation.

He hadn't even been aware that he'd fallen asleep. When Memphis woke up, he had no clue where he was or why the sun had set already. Moonlight poured onto the porch where he was still sitting lazy in the rocker. Quiet wrapped him like a blanket. Cozy. He'd never felt this relaxed in his life.

"Well now, I didn't know when you planned to wake up from that slumber, but I figured you needed it."

Memphis turned to his left to see Marie coming up some stairs toward the porch.

"It's mighty late. I best be getting on. You have been far too kind, Marie."

She stood there next to him, calm, hands clasped together.

"Moonlight is beautiful tonight. That music you played earlier would be just wonderful under her watchful eye." She pointed at the full illuminated disk in the sky, disregarding his suggestion to leave.

"But it's so quiet out here and it is rather late. I don't want to disturb anyone."

"No one will be disturbed where we are going, Memphis. Now are you gonna play for me or not?"

"I've never met a woman like you, Ms. Marie. I'm intrigued. But I don't want no trouble."

"Won't be no trouble. Unless you the trouble, Mr. Memphis. Now get that guitar and let's go."

She pointed to the corner where he had set his guitar down and he knew she meant business. Plus, curiosity killed the cat.

Memphis wasn't sure how deep they walked into the forest that was behind Marie's store. Moon was so bright, the light poured through the trees, laying a path on the ground before them as they walked in silence.

They soon came to a clearing. Darkness surrounded them like a cloak. The only light besides the moon had been a small lantern that Marie carried. She set it down on the earth. He watched as she moved about, setting down the bag she had been carrying as well. It was almost as if she floated when she moved. Memphis wasn't sure that he could see her feet actually touching the ground.

"Now, Memphis. I want you to know that things don't happen by accident. Not whatsoever. So you coming into my store was not by chance. Your soul called you there. Knew I could help. I know souls."

As Marie came closer to him, a chill ran down Memphis' spine.

"You play that guitar well, but you want more. We are out here alone, Memphis. Just you, me, the stars, and Mother Moon. Tell us what you really want."

Memphis opened his mouth to protest, but blurted out instinctively, "Money. To be rich."

"What would you do to get rich?"

He didn't know the answer to that question. "What I gotta do?"

Marie held up the lantern and for the first time, Memphis could see what was before him. Two roads, one running from East to West, one running North to South. Parallel to the East/ West road, a set a train tracks.

"It ain't about what you *gotta* do, it's about what you are willing to do."

That night, Memphis found out just how far he would go to get what he wanted. Found out that he didn't have the limits he thought he had. Under that moonlight, he found out there was freedom and infinite possibility. Filled his soul with a light that almost blinded him, yet baptized him in plenitude and a sense of knowing all at once. Magic is like that. Especially at the crossroads. There was a moment when Marie touched him, that Memphis was sure that his own feet did not touch the ground. He was sure from that point that Marie had been floating, levitating.

Ethereal.

He made covenants that night.

Under the stars.

With Marie.

Talking to Mother Moon.

When he was given the requirements, the good seemed to outweigh the bad, so he agreed.

Why wouldn't you agree to the very life you wanted if it was presented to you on a silver platter? Served up to you so seemingly easy? You weren't supposed to slam the door on opportunity when she called.

Even when she turned up by moonlight at the Devil's Playground.

~

"Ladies."

Hattie Mae went over to give greeting to a few members of the church league women's circle as she entered the general store. She watched as Pearl and Ida quickly smiled, sidestepping her as they exited the store without speaking.

"Those old rude bats!" Hattie Mae exclaimed to herself.

"Hattie Mae. I just-," Verna grabbed Hattie Mae by the arm and pulled her to the back of the store.

"Verna Toliver! What in the world is wrong with you?"

Verna smoothed her dress and straightened the strap on her purse.

"Now, I'm only going to tell you this one time, Hattie Mae. Because I consider us to be friends. But there is *talk*."

"What do you mean 'talk' Verna?"

"*Talk,*" Verna replied again through pinched lips and clenched teeth. She looked around first then continued.

"Word is, your son done gone to the Devil's Playground. That he's been seen frequenting the next town over with a conjure woman."

"Verna Toliver! Where on earth would you get that idea from? I'm offended!"

Verna scrunched her face in disbelief.

"Your fur stole here isn't offended." Verna nodded in her friend's direction, eyes fixed on the extravagant fur coat Hattie Mae was proudly wearing. "Now where did you get the money so quick, so fast to be so flashy Hattie Mae? You know people are talking."

Hattie straightened up, stoic. "My son is doing very well on the road as a traveling salesman. He's found his calling."

"Hattie Mae. You can choose to overlook things. Though, God doesn't care for that kind of avoidance of the truth."

"God also doesn't care for all this talk and gossiping and counting my pockets. Memphis has finally found something he's good at and it takes care of our family. We get a chance to have some nice things for once and I'm going to enjoy it. Thank you so much for this *talk*, Verna. Much appreciated. Give the ladies my regards."

Hattie Mae paid for her items, in full without leaving a tab, and walked home. She'd heard the talk and the gossip and the whispers. Disregarded all of it. Memphis had finally put down all that haint music and found a respectable living. He was a man. The man she always wanted him to be. People had gotten so used to her being so basic and humble, they weren't able to respect her new way of life.

She was proud of her son. He found himself and was helping his family to have a better life.

There was no way he was seeing a conjure woman or doing anything that ungodly or unsavory. She would just ask him about it when they had dinner. Settle all of this foolishness. He would be home in the next few hours, from working out of town and she could ask him then.

Or at least that was her plan, until her handsome oldest son walked in toting a fully cooked baked ham and some other fixins.

"Memphis, you know that I like to fix my own dinner."

"I know, Mama. And boy do I love your cookin'. But this is my treat. Give you a rest."

That flashy smile. Hattie Mae knew that her son could sell cayenne pepper in hell with that charisma.

"Well, since you've had this- this job, I think you've been spoilin' me way too much. And your siblings. You've been doing a wonderful job and I'm proud of you, but where are you getting all of that money from? What exactly are you selling again?"

His lips gently touched her forehead as he set the food on the table.

"Now, Mama. Don't you worry about all of that. Let me take care of things. I give you money each week to put it aside for us. I do the spending, you do the saving. Speaking of, here is a bit more."

As the younger children skipped into the kitchen, Hattie Mae tried her best to keep her composure.

But she lost that fight, snatching the bills from the hands of the younger children as her oldest son gave out prizes- gifts and money to them.

"Mama!" They all protested together.

"Your brother is over here talking about saving and here you all are wanting to spend. I will hold on to this money for you for a rainy day." She tucked the money safely in her bosom and tried to forget the fact that she had not saved one dime of the money he'd been giving her for weeks.

Saving had not been part of the discussion, although apparently, Memphis had thought it was clearly implied. Hattie Mae had simply paid the taxes on the house for the year and a few of their creditors, purchased necessities like food and such, and she'd been having a joyous time with the rest. She resolved to start saving with what he was about to give her from this point on.

And in light of the fact that she hadn't been saving, it was of no importance to g the coo any deeper into the conversation about how he really made the money he made. She wasn't working and had no alternative income, so they had to bank on all that Memphis brought in.

Memphis was it, and there was no way Hattie Mae was about to mess that up.

~

It was the most curious thing to have to walk past the church in order to get to the bar in town. Memphis was sure that had been done on purpose. When mapping out this tiny town, someone thought it a good thing to make it mandatory that you walk past the church before you went to have the good time that was on your mind.

Memphis made his way to the bar. It had been a long week and he needed to temporarily take leave of his senses and relax. Plus, if the right cook was in the back, the food was good.

The past week had been rough. He knew after the last conversation he'd had with his mother, she was not saving the money he'd given her. Part of that was his fault for not clarifying his expectation and for expecting her to be responsible with an amount of money that she'd never seen in her lifetime.

At this point, he'd been selling his oils and tinctures in all of the bordering towns and this cycle of reorders had been slow. Being a traveling salesman meant you had to have money on reserve to travel. He thought since money was slow, he could dip into the money he'd given his mother to save. His intuition told him she hadn't put one red penny to the side as she shopped and pretended not to. Memphis didn't even want to ask her how much money they had to their name.

Some things were better off left alone. Especially when you already knew the answers.

He figured instead that he would just drown his sorrows with hard, dark liquor and when he sobered up, he could create a new game plan.

"Well, well, well. If it ain't Memphis. How have you been?"

Memphis took a seat at the bar and waited for Moses, the owner and bartender to pour up a drink for him.

"Busy, man. Busy."

Moses set two shot glasses on the counter and poured the brown liquid.

"One for you. One for me," Moses said in a toast. Memphis brought his glass to the bartender's and then tossed the drink back quickly.

"Traveling from town to town is taxing."

"Can't be too much worry. That conjure woman you've been seeing surely makes it easy?"

Memphis slid the glass across the counter. "Conjure woman? Where would you have heard that, Moses?" he asked.

Moses traded the shot glass for a larger glass and gave Memphis a refill.

"Everyone is talking, man."

"Everyone?" Memphis asked, eyebrow raised.

"Everyone. Says you went a few towns over to go down to the crossroads. And we all know what happens there."

Moses busied himself wiping down the counter while Memphis got up and changed a song on the jukebox.

"Keep that glass full until I say when," he ordered.

"Whatever you say, Memphis."

It wasn't until two glasses later that Memphis decided to inquire more about what Moses was speaking of. "I'm not quite sure what happens at the crossroads. What do they say happens?"

Moses poured for a few other patrons who had shown up.

"They say a man goes down and trades his soul. Word is, you traded yours for all of this money you're making. All of this success."

"Success, hhumph." Polishing off the rest of the liquor, Memphis twirled the glass around, examining it.

"I am feeling stuck just the like the next man. Money up or down. Seems like people would mind their own business. Nothing to see here. Certainly no crossroads. And anyway, in order for that to be the word, wouldn't someone else have had to be down there at the crossroads to have seen me? You know, for truth telling and not gossip and meddlin.'"

"Well now, that's a valid point if I ever heard one. Let me pour you one more round for that."

"Maybe this round will help with my luck. People are looking at me, saying all kinds of things. But I feel like the most unlucky man in town right now."

"Perception, my brother. Perception." Moses moved on down the counter to continue serving patrons.

Perception. There was no perception. It was only people meddling and whispering.

They'd said worse about Hattie Mae's oldest son before.

Those talking weren't his customers. But there was always a small chance that the whispering was affecting his profits.

He knew exactly who could help him with that issue.

~

Stepping off the train, Memphis thought for a moment that maybe he'd made the wrong decision to come back to town and see Marie. Obviously someone was watching his moves and providing the gossip, so they would surely see his return and make sure he was the topic of conversation over the next few days.

By the time that his feet touched the ground, Memphis knew that it was too late to turn back. Marie had to have answers to why his business was slowing so quickly.

Wandering through the downtown with a mind full of thoughts, Memphis realized he had to have walked past Marie's by the time he'd gotten halfway down the main thoroughfare. He had been too engrossed in his thoughts and had obviously missed the place with the purple door. He stood there for a moment in the middle of the street, disoriented. Marie's had been next door to a florist. And there was only one florist on the block. As he approached the store front next to the florist, Memphis realized that Marie's place now looked different. The door wasn't purple. A peachy salmon color instead.

He entered a bustling space with people, smiling, talking, sipping drinks. All of the merchandise was different as well. *Maybe this is what things look like in the daytime.*

Everyone was so full of joy. Mingling. Almost floating around like Marie.

After scanning the crowd and not seeing her, Memphis decided to ask someone if she was there. And just as he did, he saw her. As he approached, he realized something about her eyes didn't look quite the same, but it had to be her.

"Marie."

Memphis called her name twice more as he walked toward her. The woman turned to him and smiled. "My name isn't Marie. Do we know each other?"

Stunned Memphis, tried to wrap his brain around what was happening.

"Uh, it's uncanny how you look like-. Well. The owner of this store. Her name is Marie. We've been acquainted and I came back to ask her a few questions. Follow up on some things we discussed the last time I was here."

The woman gently cocked her head to the side, with a smile. "I'm the owner of this store. Not sure that we've been acquainted, but I would love for you to come in and join us. Can I get you some tea, Mr.-?"

"Memphis." He extended his hand to hers, bringing her hand to his lips with a kiss. "Pleased to make your acquaintance-,"

"Terese."

"Pleased to make your acquaintance, Terese. I would love to take you up on that offer for a cup of tea." He was willing to play her little game if that was what it would take to get answers. Something strange was going on.

"My pleasure." She disappeared in the crowd, returning shortly with a small silver tray.

"You look like a peach passionflower type." She blushed while handing him a china cup.

"I will gladly take your recommendation, Terese." Their eyes met, and he couldn't deny the fact that she felt like a familiar spirit. As he lifted the cup to his lips, Memphis saw a picture on the front. A woman kneeling before the waters, blindfolded with two swords crossing her chest.

Terese saw him admiring the artwork.

"Ah, that is the Two of Swords."

"I'm not sure what you mean," Memphis replied.

"Two of Swords. In traditional tarot, it tells the tale of a person being at a crossroads of the mind. Needing to make a decision. The key here is that the water symbolizes Intuition. The suit of Swords represents the mind and a person's thoughts. She is blindfolded and almost bound by her thoughts versus using her Intuition. So when this card chooses you, it means you are at a crossroads. Needing to choose between a few major things. The thing is, the answer is typically right in front of you. You've just been too in your head to see it. I feel like this picture is symbolic of where a lot of people are often in life."

Her smile was warm, her eyes knowing. Her touch sent electricity surging through him as her hand softly brushed his arm.

"Your soul sees what it needs to see at the level where it presently lives, Memphis. But there is more to life than where you currently reside. Take the blinders off. That's the only way you will see through to where you need to go."

It was as if the words she spoke breathed life into his very being. He opened his mouth to reply, but chose to sip the rest of the tea quietly.

"I hope this trip of yours was fulfilling and not in vain, Memphis. There are a few guests I need to tend to. Perhaps we will see each other later."

Memphis nodded as Terese walked off to play gracious hostess. There was no way that he could share what had just happened here with anyone else. Partially because he didn't understand it himself.

There was also no way that he could come back here again. Something told him that this was the end of his journey here and that he would have to figure things out on his own.

~

The stroke of luck Memphis had dried up as quickly as it started. And obviously he couldn't go back to tap the well again. Marie was gone. To be honest, he had not one single clue about any of the circumstances surrounding meeting her. He wasn't even sure if that night at the crossroads had really happened. So he decided not to think of it ever again. There was no way that he would get the answers he needed or wanted.

The whispers around town had gotten too loud and his sales continued to dwindle. No one needed the tonics or oils he was selling anymore. And yet, he knew that there was no way that he could go backwards to anything he'd known before he'd become a traveling salesman. He knew that the only way out of all of this was to move forward.

Hattie Mae told him that she'd sat in her prayer closet the entire day before asking her God for answers and opportunity.

Memphis still wasn't sure if he wanted to get to know his mother's God. Still, he politely thanked her for her prayers as his mind toiled on what he was to do next.

There had to be a next.

Staying at the house with his family and his thoughts was driving him to drink, but having drinks everyday at the bar was no longer in budget. Something had to give. Or else he would have to find a place to take it from.

Maybe since he was at the bar so much, there would be an opportunity to make a couple bucks. He could surely talk to Moses and see what was on the horizon there. Putting on a tie and a shirt,

Memphis decided to make his way down to the bar. As he dressed, there was a knock at the door and he listened to see if his mother would receive who was calling on them.

He heard voices chatting and then his mother calling for him. He told her he would be down momentarily as he straightened his tie.

Entering the parlor, there was a gentleman standing there with his mother.

"Memphis, this is Mr. Charles Peters."

"Dr. Charles Peters," the man corrected.

"My apologies. Dr. Charles Peters," Hattie Mae said with a smile. "He would like to speak with you, Memphis."

Hattie Mae excused herself and left the gentleman to speak with her son.

"I am Dr. Charles Peters. A chemist and doctor of research. I will get straight to the point because time is so very valuable. Memphis, I heard that you have been selling out with a certain formula for a tonic. I would like to recreate that tonic and mass produce it. Sell it all over. Maybe rename it. Did you have a name for it?"

"I'm sorry, Dr. Charles. I'm not sure that I understand what you are saying here."

The good doctor took a moment to reiterate his proposal and wait until Memphis had processed all that was said.

"Now, I can either buy you out for the formula or you can come and work for me as the dynamic salesman you are and make a hefty sized commission, plus have partnership in the business. I have written some figures here for you to consider."

Memphis felt his legs almost go weak when he examined the financial offer. "You are willing to pay for my formula?"

His mouth went dry with excitement.

"I am. But as I said, this is a business proposal. You should take some time to talk it over with your family. That part is important. This is quite a decision to make."

Crossroads.

Decisions.

More decisions.

The figures presented were quite substantial and this would be life changing. Memphis thanked the doctor, knowing immediately what deal he would take, but asking for another moment to think things over.

He stared at Dr. Charles' handwriting. The phone number neatly printed under the proposal offer along with the address to where the doctor would be staying while he was there in town on business.

"God has worked this all out for us, Memphis. I just know it."

Memphis turned to see his mother standing beside him.

"God, you say?"

She gently placed a hand on his shoulder. "I sat in my prayer closet all day yesterday, praying for a miracle. And then today, Dr. Charles knocks on our door with an offer. By the way, what was the offer exactly?"

Memphis glanced at the paper and then stuffed it in his pocket for safe keeping. His mother didn't need to know the exact figures.

"The prayer closet brought this offer, you figure? Not my hard work, but what you did in the prayer closet?"

"Oh Chile," Hattie Mae sighed. "God is always out here working for us. Let's just be thankful that we were home when opportunity came knocking. I hope you speak with Dr. Charles soon."

Memphis watched as his mother walked off toward the kitchen.

Opportunity had knocked. Practically made the decision for him.

Memphis felt that God hadn't been interested in him at all until he went down to the crossroads. Opportunity had been interested in him though.

And he had not one regret about answering Opportunity and all that it would bring when he would speak with the doctor and give his final decision. Chance and Luck showed up as Opportunity's acquaintance, and Memphis wasn't going to let any of them pass him by.

A Word On Secrets

A Word on Secrets

Our families hold secrets. Gifts unleashed only in the dark. Hidden, sometimes in plain sight. Fed quietly by the fears, guilt, and shame carried by generations. It's never enough to satiate it. Secrets need plenty of nourishment. Those secrets soon feed on souls. Draining them of sustenance. Siphoning their dignity and feeding dearly on any ability toward happiness and peace.

We find reasons to feed the beast. Reasons to keep that beast fat, gluttonous. All at the sake of ourselves and somehow in the name of martyrdom. When that day comes where we open the windows in the attic, asking sunlight and fresh air to pour in, the beast roars, burned by the sun's warmth. Those secrets hidden so long, the very sound of them on our lips creates a frequency that is deafening and we beg for quiet again.

At any cost.

We need that silence. We need that volume turned down. So we rush to feed the beast. Tame it so he will continue to hide. Problem is, someone has to commit to the nurture and care of the beast over the years. Over years and decades. And even as the generations that initiated and cultivated it return to the ethers.

Gatekeepers. Guardians. It's funny how those concepts are usually revered but also apply to those that maintain the secrets.

When and how will they ever see the light of day? Who would be the gatekeeper when they do?

Sins Of The Father

Sins Of The Father

Sins of the Father
Silence
The death blow
Drains the very vitality
Generations die over and over
Voices repeatedly suffocating
Unable to breathe the stifling air of the atmosphere
Memories erased
Purposely forgotten
Names unknown
Although pieces of life that remain haunt us in this realm
So many secrets
How do we tiptoe by our past?
Whisper taboos in the shadows?
Ancestors only stay quiet for so long
Truth can't lie buried but for a moment
Life so far, floating recklessly on the wind
Unplanted
That earth beneath our feet soon becomes pliable
Soil rich with lies only bears rotten fruit
Divine wisdom shines the light
Illumination by the power of the Full Moon
Sins of the father
Preserves the very chaos that has fed our souls for this eternity

Reincarnating us with karmic memories that slowly kill us from our first breath

3

Revelation

The sky had been orange that morning. Like burning flames enveloping the sky. The child was convinced that the sky was close enough to touch her, scorch her in fact and she insisted that they not hurry off to market at their normal time. Her mother decided it would be okay to go to the market a little later than usual. She set about making some warm milk sprinkled with cinnamon for her young daughter, who seemed to be more and more sensitive to weather changes and the color of the sky. Whatever would bring calm to the child, especially since she was in no rush in particular.

By the time the horizon turned the most beautiful shade of blue, the young child had grabbed her cloak and a basket and waited by the front door of the cottage for her mother.

"Selena my darling. Whatever will I do with you?" Mother asked gently as she caressed her daughter's face.

"I was just trying to follow the instructions the woman gave me last night. She said not to walk the main road under the light of the bursting Sun. Something about minds separating from bodies."

Mother gasped. "Selena. My child. Your imagination is much too active for a child your age."

"But, Mother." The child looked into her mother's eyes and paused the conversation.

"My heart speaks with yours and I already know what you are about to say, Child. And yes, you have been correct on all prophecies. This one seems a bit-," Her mother paused and then left them walking in silence for at least a mile. The dreams that came to Selena were always correct, but usually came in riddles and metaphors that initially left them baffled.

"Mother, what is that up ahead?"

A young man came riding up to them by horse.

"Pardon me. This area is closed. You must use the alternate passage through the west."

Selena and Mother looked to the path in the west.

"Kind Sir. That is the longer path. We are going to market and already late this morning. Is there no way down the normal path?"

The man sat stoic on his horse. "There is not this morning. A tragedy has happened. One of a gruesome sort. It is best that women and children not see. It is rather late in the morning. The carriage here awaits as a ride for those who are feeble. But in light of all that has happened in this tragedy, the closing of the main road, and the fact that you remind me of my own dear mother, I will have the carriage carry you off to market. It would be a shame for you not to receive your daily rations."

Mother thanked the man for his kindness as she and Selena boarded the carriage. The driver explained that there was a covering over the window for protection and modesty as they started down the path and that it was best that it remained lowered.

The covering offered visual protection, but did not protect their ears from hearing some of the men talking. Mother covered Selena's ears as the men discussed how to properly dispose of bodies with severed heads and how the entire sight of it all looked to be the workings of some other worldly beings because a slaughter of that magnitude could not have been accomplished by a simple man.

Once they arrived in the market, there was a calm, despite the happenings on their ride over. Selena was always happy to run around freely. All of the sights and sounds were exhilarating to her. The scent of food, the sight of women dressed so beautifully selling their finest wares. She hoped her mother would buy her some of the candies she loved so much.

Selena promised her mother that she would meet her shortly near the north entrance vendors so they could pick fruit. There was so much to see and do in the market and the loudness and constant chaos of it all was stark contrast to their quiet, neat home life.

"Child, come to me."

Selena turned around to see a frail, cloaked woman beckoning to her. A bony finger called out to the child, who turned around to see if her mother was in sight. She was not immediately close, and this woman felt very familiar.

"You are the one that has the dreams. The one that will bring the prophecy to life."

"Me?" Selena asked, eyeing the woman curiously. "Are you-?"

"Selena, who is this you are talking to?" The child felt her mother grab her and pull her close.

"This is the woman from my dreams, Mother. The one who told me about the separating of the mind from the body and the orange skies. This is her!"

Mother could not be equally excited. "This is my child. I will take it very kindly if you mind yourself elsewhere."

The woman reached for the child gently, and then pulled back. "She has the prophecy. The gift. There is no ignoring the messages that God will send her. No ignoring. Nurture the gift."

Mother grabbed Selena's hand in a tight grip and pulled the child into her chest. "She is a child. My child. I don't know who you are, but please leave us alone. Selena, let's go."

"Oh, but this is the child that saw the beginning of the reckoning. She saw the fowl in the air falling and reported such. People came from far and wide to sit at her feet, but you moved away. You can't run from God's calling on your life, dear. Your calling is intertwined with hers. Your job is to let her be who God called her to be, not to let your fears impede her gifts. She is an Oracle and is to be a blessing to so many others."

A small crowd had started to gather.

"That's enough!" Mother shrieked. She began to pull her child away from where they stood with the old woman, yet the old woman still cried out.

"There will be four dreams that come to her. She is to preach the prophecy as she sees it. Mankind has a job to listen and take heed. Four dreams, dear. Please remember." The woman continued speaking even though Mother and Selena were rushing away in the other direction.

The entire way home, Mother reminded Selena how she warned her over and over not to speak with strangers. Reminded her that their quiet life was the goal and that she could not go out drawing attention to herself in the way that she had done today.

Selena simply nodded, wanting her mother to find peace. Besides, she'd done nothing but walk around the marketplace, in search of tasty treats. She'd done nothing wrong. But she knew at this moment, her mother's fear would not let her see that fact and accept it. Her mother had been fiercely trying to protect her her entire life.

In her prayers that night, Selena asked for protection and guidance. The dreams would come whether she wanted them to or not.

1

Selena opened her eyes. It was to no avail because all around her was black. A void of sorts. There was nothing. She stood there simply listening to the sound of her breath. It was the only sound, besides her heart beating. It didn't feel like calling out to any in particular would matter. There was no one else there with her. The darkness was strangely comforting and she felt no immediate desire to move. She didn't want to miss anything.

A breeze tickled her skin in the softest way. It felt safe and familiar, just as a bit of light began to creep in. A beautiful white aura floated over to her. Quietly, Selena's soul connected with the energy, letting the message download in her spirit. When she looked to her left, Selena was aware of another calming presence. It appeared to be a woman, cloaked in soft white with a blue sash tied at the waist of her robe. She simply held her hand out to Selena, who instinctively knew to take it.

A sudden wailing moaning came from nowhere and was beyond deafening. Guttural. When Selena opened her eyes, there was brightness. A knight in all black armor rode past her, almost in slow motion. He didn't seem to acknowledge that Selena stood there with the angel. His presence faded out as soon as he rode past. The angel held her hand out, pointing in encouragement for Selena to step away from her. For the first time, Selena felt afraid as the angel nudged her.

The moaning rose again, in waves. She could not tell where it was coming from specifically. The sounds seemed to come from all over, all at once penetrating the vacuum she was initially in. The ground beneath her feet began to shake as the knight rode back toward her at full speed, so fast that she didn't have time to move. Selena braced herself as she absorbed his energy as he rode past her. The ground swelled, a fissure forming along the path the knight rode. As he stopped in front of her, she was able to see more closely.

He opened his breastplate and the volume of the moaning and wailing increased. Suddenly around her, people were dying. People lie on the ground writhing in pain, pleading. The sun became hot, scorching. Deep in the pit of her soul, Selena felt hunger pangs. Her throat went dry and her knees buckled as she reached out for the angel, who seemed further and further away. She had no voice, despite wanting to scream. People dropped where they stood, after staggering. After crying out for help. And after they fell to the arid ground, a larger fissure opened as buildings sprang up and then towers crumbled.

Selena was on her knees, holding her own throat, gasping for air. Reaching for the angel.

The knight raised his face mask and Selena searched for his eyes. Nothingness was potent but suddenly she found her breath as she fell completely to the ground.

The knight towered over her as she lay on the ground that shook relentlessly as it began opening up. Swallowing the moans. Swallowing all of the wails and the crying, returning souls to the ethers.

The Knight closed his breastplate, raised his sword, and with a sonic shriek, he rode off, just as quickly as he had appeared.

Selena's cries broke through as sound welled up in her throat from someplace deep. It was a necessary release. As she lay there, still on the ground, tears formed in her eyes as she looked around for her angel. The angel was near and beckoned to her. There were no words. Nothing to say. Only a knowing.

Selena had her first visit. There were to be three more.

2

The next night, as Selena closed her eyes, she prayed that she would have the strength to get through the rest of the visits. The first prophecy had been so real, she awakened shaking and unable to focus. She didn't want to tell her mother of the dreams, or that it was happening just as the woman told them it would. Mother would be rattled beyond belief. Instead, when she awakened, she wrote down all that she'd experienced and tucked it away.

Closing her eyes to drift off to sleep was no small feat. Once she did, she found herself in a sea of red. Bright crimson all around her. It was as if the world was on fire. Burning. Everywhere she stepped, the ground was smoldering, smoke rising from every crevice. She quickly thought to look for an angel. One had appeared the last time and surely there would be one to guide her this time around.

She quietly stood to take a look at all that was happening around her. Closed her eyes to absorb all that she felt. The heat. The scent of flesh burning. The sounds of horns blaring. She could practically taste the cinders in the air. She opened her eyes to see someone coming her way. It was as if the figure was moving quickly and in slow motion at the same time. The words spoken were unintelligible, but the moans and cries were a signal that something was amiss.

The figure stopped in front of where Selena stood. She was not sure if it was male or female. They were small in stature, stout, clad in a red robe that trailed behind them. A floppy red hat on their head and dark eyes that seemed to look through Selena instead of at her or in her direction.

They reached behind them and pulled out a horn with their right hand, and there among the flames, played a warning sound. A scroll suddenly appeared in their left hand, and opened on its own.

The flames rose and lowered as if in waves as the figure spoke.

It is hereby official proclamation by the court of the King that we announce the King's death

His death occurred approximately one hour ago and was confirmed by the court physician. With no immediate heir, the throne is now in threat for succession as the next of kin has been clear in their desire not to take the throne. Our country now prepares for war in the name of the King as his succession line switches and the people are unprotected. May his kingdom ever reign. God rest his soul. God have mercy on the inhabitants of this country.

As the figure rolled up the scroll, it disappeared as suddenly as it had appeared. They blew the horn and turned in Selena's direction. Blank eyes and a sly grin, all of a sudden the figure split into two right before her eyes.

The two figures were identical. Selena watched in awe as they danced around in a circle, kicking up their feet while singing among the flames. They appeared to be teasing one another and arguing.

You killed the King!

I did not! You killed the King!

I did not! He deserved to die though. Thought he knew every-thing. Never listening to anyone. Couldn't hear anyone over his own loud voice.

I didn't kill the King!

Yes you did! And it's okay. Someone had to do it. It all had to fall down. Crumble. He had to die. If you hadn't done it, I would have done it. Killed the King.

Who will wear the Lion on their breastplate now? Who is in charge of the Sun rising and setting? Who will wear the crown and rule?

You killed the King! What if he died and no one ruled? What if everyone rules themselves? Would they all come together?

You killed the King! And you knew when you did it, someone else would come to rule. That's the way it has to be. But we will soon forget about this King. Will soon focus on another just the same.

You did kill the King!

I know. I killed the King!

The two danced a jig, held hands frolicking in a circle, laughing maniacally. Selena was ready to leave this place. The heat was becoming consuming. Her angel hadn't arrived. She'd watched this all on her own. Yet she'd known with discernment that she was safe.

The figures continued singing while it all burned to the ground.

Do you think she sees us?

Of course she does. And she's heard every word we said. She will tell them that it all has to burn. Die. All of it.

The flames rose as the pair stopped dancing, turned to Selena and looked directly at her. One of them took the horn and pointed it at her, blew it, sending her right back into the waking realm.

3

The third night, Selena's vision was baptized in blue. The cerulean scene was both serene and terrifying all at once. There was one more dream after this one to endure. Selena closed her eyes and said a prayer. Hoping this time, her angel would show up. Help her to see what she needed to see.

Her prayer was not to avoid any of what was happening, but to have the ability to endure the assignment. Birds were tweeting, and suddenly, the Sun was shining. She felt, for a moment, that she would be able to have clarity for whatever was going to occur next. A field of flowers bloomed immediately nearby where she stood. The beautiful scent drifted on the warm breeze, wrapping Selena in a feeling of calm.

An angel appeared, beckoning for Selena to follow her. The two walked in the field of the flowers, which at this point seemed endless against the horizon. Selena followed quietly, not wanting to miss anything she may need to see or experience. Eventually, they came upon a small clearing with a blue wrought iron bench. The sunlight seemed to be brighter in that space. Holding her hand out, the Angel showed the way for Selena to move forward. Doing as she was asked, Selena moved closer to the brightest spot where the Sun touched the ground. Suddenly, a beautiful woman appeared in the clearing. Selena was drawn to her energy and she did not refuse her desire to walk over to the woman and fall at her feet.

Once there on the ground in front of her, the flowers were in full bloom again against the backdrop of the sky, which had now changed to the cerulean color Selena had seen once the dream first started. Stars began to appear in the sky and the Moon hung bright and bold. The angel beckoned for Selena to come and stand by her side. Moonlight bathed the opening where the women stood. Selena watched as slowly, people started to come from seemingly nowhere and drop to the woman's feet, just as Selena had done.

The woman handed each of them a small blue box. Selena watched as each of the first people opened the box. Light illuminated their faces and they appeared as if they had seen a miracle. Selena continued to watch as each of the people gave the woman back the box she had given to them. Only a few pleasantly kept the box they were given, reciprocating with thanks and praise. Those that kept the box were able to walk away with beautiful flowers from the garden.

Selena looked around, only to find it was just her and the woman standing there eye to eye, bathed in the moonlight. The girl child looked to her angel for confirmation. The angel urged her to take her turn. Selena fell to her feet. The woman handed her a blue box, just as she'd handed to the others. Taking a deep breath, she opened the box without hesitation.

The beauty and splendor of what happened next was hard to put into words for the girl. She simply closed her eyes and absorbed it all. The sounds, the aura, the Love and the Light. It felt like a gift that was made to give wholeness and abundance. It was something she didn't feel she could turn away. It felt like a privilege, one that Selena did not want to take for granted.

When she opened her eyes, the splendor of the garden stretched out toward the horizon and there was no one there but her. Silence blanketed everything. Her heart beating was the only sound she heard. Her breath was the energy that brought her back to center. She felt full and the urge to share came over her.

There, under the moonlight, in a sea of blue, Selena knew that there was no turning back. Only moving forward into a great unknown.

4

On the last night, Selena knelt before her bed and silently said a prayer. She asked that her angels surround and support her as she received the last vision. This last vision would bring things full circle.

Selena lay there in the darkness and listened to the sound of her mother walking around the house, praying her early morning prayer. The scent of jasmine and sandalwood burning drifted into her room. A comfort. By the time the bells chimed, she knew that the early morning hours had arrived and sleep had evaded her. Dawn was on the horizon.

At some point, her mother had gone to rest until the sun rose, as she did every morning after her prayer. Selena closed her eyes, patiently waiting. There were four dreams and the fourth had not arrived, but she knew that it would.

As she lay there, listening to the rhythm of her own heart, she heard a rustling and was aware of a presence. Out of the darkness, a small white light shone. A dot in the sea of darkness. Selena focused on the speck, covering her eyes as it grew. The warm light cradled her. Enveloped her. Shielding her eyes, she tried to see what was in front of her.

Nothing but a sea of white light.

"Selena, my child. Come to me."

As her vision came into focus, the brightness swirled around her in an aura. An orb floating in her field of vision.

"Come to me, child."

Selena stood up and followed the orb obediently. Her steps ordered. Her feet softly taking each step with a mustard seed sized faith. In that sea of white, Selena basked, absorbed. Vibrations and frequencies abound. Whispers echoed and filled her as she continued toward the orb. The visions she was given felt sacred. Appreciation filled her as she knew that she was being given something priceless. Something that was not entrusted to anyone else.

As the light grew smaller, she said another prayer of thanks as the darkness washed in and the light returned to the tiny dot. Silence was all around her. In her hand were soft white flower petals that fell to the ground as she revealed her palm with a strange marking.

When the Sun rose, Selena knew by the look on her mother's face, when she revealed the marking, that they were on the way to see the priest. There was no other place to find answers.

5

The Priest and Divine Assignments

By the time Selena and her mother reached the village, they were met with a sea of people surrounding the church.

"Mother, what is happening?"

Selena's mother squeezed her daughter's hand tightly, pulling the child into her bosom as they tried to push through the crowd.

"The child is here! The prophet has arrived!" There was a collective gasp as they turned in Selena's direction. People whispered, staring. Selena found comfort in her mother's embrace as people started closing in around her.

"Everyone, stand back. Give the child and her mother some space." The voice was commanding and the firmness comforting. Selena peeked from behind her mother's cloak to see the Priest standing on the marble steps of the church. His open arms extended.

She glanced at Mother as she ushered her up the steps. Once they reached where the Priest stood, some of the other men of the cloth closed in around them, forming a sort of shield.

"Now, everyone! We must give the child and her mother some space. Please! They are here to do God's work and we must give them grace in order to do that work. They deserve space to carry out the assignment God has given them, just as anyone else is deserving."

The sea receded at his command. People waited quietly, some crying in prayer, some bowing.

"Word has spread quickly that a child would come to give word of four prophecies. It came to me and we kept vigil and waited all night for the child to come at dawn after the fourth night. People began to take notice and came to pray with me. Waiting for a word. And here you are, just as the word guided. Come child, share with me the prophecy. We will go inside and pray as you share the word. We will confer with God before we share with the world.

The Priest led the way into the church, followed by a few of the clergy. Selena jumped, startled at the sound of the bolts being laid on the door.

"Dear child, I will not ask many questions. We will go back to the public and let God do all of the work. I simply want to be sure that you understand you have been asked to step into a purpose larger than most will ever receive in a lifetime. I also ask your mother, I ask if the two of you are ready for what life looks like when God uses you to give words and blessings to mankind?"

Selena sat quietly, waiting for her mother to protest. Instead, she watched as tears fell from Mother's eyes. The priest handed Mother a handkerchief and took her hand, reciting a prayer. He blessed them bothe and covered them with communion before they all went back outside.

A silence fell over the crowd as the Priest stepped forward.

"Five mornings ago, I awoke to a tremendous sunrise. The sky was orange, like a flame burning. For some reason, it felt like there was no boundary between the Heavens and our existence here on Earth. On that morning, I received the word from Archangel Metatron, that there would be a child that would receive prophecies over the course of the next four nights. She would come to the church after those prophecies were given, looking for answers, confirmation, and refuge.

"She is a pure representation of God's light. Her own light, untouched and not vexed by the recklessness, the heaviness of the world. She does not live life jaded or with burden and therefore, is the right vessel to receive the Prophecy which will change us and encourage us to change the world.

"There are many things that need change, transformation, as far as mankind is concerned. And I was told that a girl child would have the answers, straight from God.

"I was also told that we would know her in confirmation by three things.

"She would appear with her raven haired mother. The child would come bearing white flower petals that will fall to the earth as feathers from the Heavens. There will be a mark on her left hand in this shape."

He held up a paper with a geometrical shape centered on the page.

Selena felt the ground under her feet moving, as if she could not keep her balance. When she saw the shape on the paper, she instinctively reached for it.

Gasps and shrieks as the white flower petals she had been holding in a pocket closest to her breast fell to the ground. She looked around her as the petals continued to fall softly. She had not remembered there being so many, but as she stared, the ground around her was covered.

"Does she have the mark?" someone yelled from the crowd.

"May I?" the Priest asked.

Selena gave him her left hand. Holding her wrist, he encouraged her to open her hand, exposing her palm with the geometric shape. People began to fall to their knees in prayer.

"And the last sign of confirmation." The Priest turned to Mother. The woman let the hood of her cloak fall to her shoulders, revealing the raven colored hair.

A collective gasp rolled through the crowd, followed by tears and rejoicing.

The Priest did his best to calm the crowd before he continued to speak. "Over the next few days, we will see to it that the prophecy revealed to this child will be recorded. We will write every word and rejoice on the next sabbath at sundown."

And rejoice they did. There was a feast held in honor of the prophecy. The Feast of the White Roses was marked as a commemorative day. A day in which the child prophet came forward and spoke of the four apocalyptic dreams she was given. Messages from God that would help mankind to do better in communion with one another. Messages of healing that reminded humans of their flaws and that no matter what, God would be there to make a way out of no way, and to lead and guide those who were open to leadership, Divine Guidance, and Divine Assignment.

An Introduction
To Light

~1

An Introduction to Light

Alluring wastelands
Souls wandering
Scavenging
Searching
Lost
They live in wanderlust, yet so unfulfilled
Driven to the brink of everything and nothing all at once
Somewhere out there a parallel universe exists
One where souls no longer answer cravings
The wasteland lacks magic
Someone turned out the lights and made hiding in the shadows
fashionable
Told you that darkness was synonymous with all the evils of
this realm
So when those evils approach you in the daylight
You quickly make acquaintance
Takes nothing more than a handshake and smile

Evil doesn't have to work too hard
Because you only expect it to show up in the darkness
So much so, you live perilously in the light
Thinking you've won because you sidestep and avoid the shadows
They know all of your aversions
So they hide your magic in the darkness
Tuck it away nicely with all of the things you said you would never do
Alluring wastelands
Created in the light
Convinced you that the illuminated road ahead was an obstacle instead of salvation
Told you that Knowledge and Truth is your enemy
Making it difficult to ascend
Transformation lies dormant and untouched
Everything remains as is
Beautiful epiphanies in purgatory
Stagnant in the void
Power dormant in the darkness
Planted and unfertilized
When did you decide to settle in?
Rebuking the elevation
Denying your power and your birth rite
Especially when you have all that you need to transcend
Came into this life with all that is necessary
You don't need permission to live and breathe
But you live in the wastelands, unfed and unsatisfied
The shadows keep calling
Your magic is calling
Awakenings occurred in the parallel
Transcendence and Elevation are required

An Introduction
To Joy

An Introduction To Joy

The Tower moment occurred
It all came crashing down
A house of cards built on a foundation of quicksand
The fall was inevitable
Hearts cry out for all that will be left behind
There aren't many pieces that should be picked up
Sifted out of the ashes to be re-examined
How many times should it all be analyzed
Intellectualized
Living in the present existence was never infinite
The Tower moment came just when it should
The collapse
The inevitable fall
And when it is all leveled
Cleared
Burned to the ground
When the silence takes over

The one moment among the smoldering ashes
When one wonders what will be
That should be the moment when there is no turning back
Acceptance and Pivots
When the Sun rises from the East
The path will be new
The fear will be real
The faith will be necessary
New directions as the Phoenix rises
Unafraid of the light
She's been burned before
No more living in the past
Rebirth lies ahead
Light is a supernatural phenomenon
The future is calling
We live again after The Tower crumbles
This time, the foundation is Joy

An Introduction To Progression

~3

An Introduction to Progression

None of this is comfortable
At this point, it feels like we've started over a million times
Progression is one step in front of the other
Requirements to move forward
We can no longer hide the ugly truths
Buried beneath the surface
Yet, in plain sight
We can no longer continue to bond with the past
Paying tribute to only the familiar
We've come through
Journeying
There is no looking back
Even when the road ahead is paved with doubt
Laced in fear
Uproot it all
Turn over the soil fertilized in blood
Which has spent centuries harvesting the half dead

Progression can't involve resurrection from that soil
Incarnation is the next step
Transcending frequencies into a new realm
Moving forward
Breathing life into the fibers of being
A new existence
Decide the road ahead is paved with the intentionality of possibilities
Expansion on the horizon
Milk & Honey won't sustain this lifetime
Our souls require more
DNA rewired
Transformation beneath the surface
Healing starts from within

Photography by
Chiajuanna Holden

Tamara Angela loves writing and lives in Atlanta where she is a mother of two children and is a Reiki practitioner and works with people through mindfulness techniques to help support others in their personal therapeutic development. She loves reading just as much as writing and is an avid Danielle Steele and J California Cooper fan. She also has a passion for indulging in red velvet cupcakes and red lipstick. She writes and releases short stories on her blog The Black Southern Gothic Mystic on Substack and is a fan of any show or movie with a southern gothic aesthetic.